GW01158166

ASOGWA JUSTINA

The Idea Explorers: Adventures in Creativity

Copyright © 2024 by Asogwa Justina

All rights reserved. No part of this publication may be reproduced, stored or transmitted in any form or by any means, electronic, mechanical, photocopying, recording, scanning, or otherwise without written permission from the publisher. It is illegal to copy this book, post it to a website, or distribute it by any other means without permission.

Asogwa Justina asserts the moral right to be identified as the author of this work.

Asogwa Justina has no responsibility for the persistence or accuracy of URLs for external or third-party Internet Websites referred to in this publication and does not guarantee that any content on such Websites is, or will remain, accurate or appropriate.

First edition

This book was professionally typeset on Reedsy.
Find out more at reedsy.com

Contents

1

The Mysterious Artifact

The air was thick with dust, a tangible veil that clung to everything like an old secret. As the sun dipped below the horizon, casting long shadows through the broken windows of the abandoned library, Professor Eliza Thornfield adjusted her flashlight. The beam cut through the gloom, illuminating stacks of forgotten tomes and ancient manuscripts that lined the towering shelves. The silence was profound, broken only by the occasional creak of wood or the whisper of a breeze.

Eliza's breath fogged up the lens of her glasses as she scanned the room. She had ventured into this forsaken place on a hunch—a lead from an obscure journal she had found tucked away in a rare bookshop. The journal had hinted at a hidden treasure within this very library, a treasure that, according to legend, could unlock the greatest secrets of creativity. Her colleagues, skeptical of her pursuits, had stayed behind, leaving her to uncover the truth alone.

The beam of her flashlight caught a glint of something metallic nestled between two dusty volumes. Curious, Eliza brushed off the layers of dust, revealing a small, ornate box. The box was intricately carved with symbols she didn't recognize—interlocking patterns and mysterious runes that seemed to shimmer faintly in the dim light. Her heart quickened as she carefully pried it open with her gloved hands.

Inside the box lay a curious object: a crystal orb, suspended within a delicate metal cage. The orb seemed to pulse with a faint, ethereal light, casting eerie shadows that danced across the walls. Eliza's fingers trembled as she lifted the orb from its resting place. It felt warm to the touch, as though it had been waiting for centuries to be discovered.

As she examined the orb, a sudden gust of wind howled through the library, sending a shiver down her spine. The temperature dropped noticeably, and the orb's glow intensified, casting a haunting light that flickered and wavered. Eliza turned sharply, her flashlight revealing nothing but the encroaching darkness beyond the library's shelves. She felt an unsettling presence, an awareness that she was not alone.

With a deep breath, Eliza carefully placed the orb back into the box, closing it with a decisive snap. The whispering wind ceased abruptly, leaving an oppressive silence in its wake. She gathered her courage and stepped towards the library's exit, her footsteps echoing ominously through the grand hall.

Suddenly, a loud crash reverberated through the library, making Eliza jump. The sound came from the back of the building, where the shelves were collapsing under an unseen weight. Heart racing, she turned and hurried toward the noise. Her flashlight beam swept across toppled books and scattered debris, revealing a hidden door partially obscured by fallen bookshelves. It had been concealed for years, its presence unknown until now.

Eliza pried open the door with difficulty, the hinges groaning in protest. Beyond it lay a narrow, winding staircase descending into darkness. Without hesitation, she descended the steps, her flashlight piercing the blackness. The air grew colder with each step, and the walls seemed to close in, creating a claustrophobic sensation.

At the bottom of the staircase, Eliza found herself in a cavernous chamber, its walls lined with shelves full of arcane scrolls and artifacts. In the center of the room stood a pedestal, upon which rested an ancient, leather-bound tome. The book's cover was adorned with the same mysterious symbols she had seen on the box. It seemed to pulse with an almost palpable energy.

Eliza approached the pedestal, her curiosity overpowering her apprehension. As she reached out to touch the book, the room was suddenly bathed in an eerie green light. Shadows twisted and coiled around her, forming unsettling shapes that seemed to move of their own accord. Her flashlight flickered wildly, casting sporadic beams that failed to pierce the suffocating darkness.

A low, guttural growl echoed through the chamber, sending a jolt of fear through Eliza. She spun around, searching for the source of the sound, but saw nothing. The growl came again, closer this time, as if something unseen was stalking her.

Eliza's breath came in short, sharp gasps as she fought to keep her composure. Her fingers trembled as she grabbed the book, feeling the ancient leather beneath her fingertips. As she lifted it, the growl turned into a roar, and the shadows surged toward her.

Panicking, Eliza dashed back toward the staircase, the book clutched tightly to her chest. The chamber seemed to warp and shift around her, making it difficult to find her way. She stumbled up the stairs, the roar growing louder and more insistent, echoing off the walls and reverberating in her bones.

Reaching the top of the staircase, Eliza burst through the hidden door and into the library, only to find that the room was no longer as she had left it. The shelves were now in disarray, and the air was charged with a palpable sense of danger. The orb's glow from the box had dimmed, but the feeling of being watched was more intense than ever.

Eliza backed away slowly, her mind racing as she tried to make sense of what she had just experienced. The library's once-familiar surroundings now seemed alien and hostile. As she turned to leave, the orb's faint glow flickered one last time, casting a final, unsettling shadow that seemed to whisper of secrets yet to be uncovered.

With a final glance at the enigmatic artifact, Eliza fled the library, her heart pounding in her chest. The mystery of the orb and the tome had only just begun to unravel, and she knew that the true adventure was only beginning.

2

The Enigmatic Map

Eliza's car screeched to a halt as she swerved into the gravel driveway of her modest countryside home. The library's secrets weighed heavily on her mind, and her pulse had not yet returned to normal since her frantic escape. With trembling hands, she grabbed the small, ornate box from the passenger seat and hurried inside. The orb, now safely enclosed within, had already begun to feel like a beacon drawing her into an unknown destiny.

Inside her cluttered study, Eliza carefully placed the box on her desk, her fingers still shaking from the adrenaline. The room was filled with stacks of papers, open books, and various research materials scattered about. She pulled her chair closer to the desk and took a deep breath, trying to steady herself. The artifact's mysterious symbols and the eerie occurrences in the library replayed in her mind.

With deliberate movements, she opened the box and took out the orb, setting it on the desk before her. Its faint glow seemed to pulse in rhythm with her heartbeat, casting erratic shadows on the walls. Next, she retrieved the leather-bound tome from her bag and laid it on the desk. The book was ancient, its cover adorned with intricate symbols similar to those on the orb and the box.

Eliza's fingers traced the patterns on the book as she flipped it open to the first page. It was written in a language she did not recognize, but there were illustrations of fantastical maps and diagrams that seemed to depict a realm of shifting landscapes and bizarre structures. The text was a mixture of cryptic symbols and archaic script, each page more enigmatic than the last.

After hours of deciphering, she finally came across a page with a map. The map was detailed, showing a labyrinthine network of tunnels and caverns, but the locations were marked with symbols that matched the ones on the orb. A note scrawled in the margin hinted at a "hidden path" and "unveiling the truth," suggesting that the map was not just a guide but a key to something much more profound.

Eliza's excitement was palpable. She decided to take a closer look at the orb, convinced it might hold additional clues. As she examined it, the glow seemed to intensify, and the symbols on its surface began to rearrange themselves. The orb was clearly more than a mere artifact—it was a part of a larger puzzle.

Her concentration was abruptly broken by a sudden knock at the door. Eliza's heart raced as she glanced at the clock—far too late for casual visitors. Hesitantly, she approached the door and peered through the peephole. Outside, a shadowy figure stood on her doorstep. She could make out little more than a dark silhouette, but the figure's presence sent a chill down her spine.

With a cautious sigh, Eliza opened the door. Standing there was a tall man in a long coat, his face partially obscured by a wide-brimmed hat. His eyes were hidden behind dark glasses, and his demeanor was unsettlingly calm. He held out a small envelope, which he claimed contained information pertinent to her recent discovery.

Eliza hesitated before taking the envelope. The man did not offer any explanation and simply nodded before turning and walking away into the night. As she closed the door, she examined the envelope closely. It was unmarked, with only her name written in a precise, formal script. The weight of the envelope felt oddly heavy, and the edges were crisp, as though it had just been sealed.

Sitting back at her desk, Eliza carefully opened the envelope and extracted a single sheet of paper. The paper was aged and fragile, and it bore a hand-drawn map—eerily similar to the one in the tome, but with additional markings and annotations. The new map highlighted specific locations within the labyrinth, pointing out areas of interest with cryptic symbols and warnings.

Eliza's pulse quickened as she studied the new map. It indicated a starting point that seemed to align with the location of the library where she had found the orb. The annotations on the map suggested that the hidden path would be activated only when certain conditions were met. She felt a surge of anticipation mixed with apprehension.

Just as she began to analyze the implications of the map, another loud knock echoed through the house. Startled, Eliza grabbed a flashlight and moved cautiously toward the door. Her thoughts raced—was the visitor connected to the shadowy figure from earlier?

This time, she peered through the peephole again. To her shock, the figure from before was back, but this time, he was accompanied by another person. Both wore dark clothing and seemed to be scanning the surroundings intently.

Eliza decided to avoid opening the door. Instead, she watched through a nearby window as the two figures huddled together, speaking in low, urgent tones. Their presence was unsettling, and Eliza couldn't shake the feeling that they were somehow connected to the mysterious events unfolding around her.

The two figures eventually left, their departure as sudden and stealthy as their arrival. Eliza's mind was awash with questions and fears. The enigmatic map, the shadowy visitors, and the increasingly sinister aura surrounding the orb all pointed toward a deeper conspiracy.

With resolve hardening in her chest, Eliza returned to her desk. She meticulously examined the map and its annotations, comparing them with the symbols on the orb and the leather-bound tome. It was clear that her journey was far from over. The hidden path and the labyrinth were calling her, and she knew that unraveling the mystery would demand everything she had.

As the night deepened and the shadows lengthened, Eliza prepared herself for the adventure ahead. The answers lay somewhere within the labyrinth, waiting to be discovered. With a final glance at the enigmatic map, she steeled herself for whatever challenges lay ahead. The game was afoot, and Eliza was determined to uncover the truth, no matter the cost.

3

The Lost City of Dreams

**Chapter 3:

   The moon hung low in the sky, casting a silvery glow over the dense forest that stretched endlessly before Eliza. The air was cool and crisp, carrying a whisper of unease as she trekked through the underbrush, her flashlight cutting a narrow path through the darkness. The ancient map had led her here, to a hidden city long forgotten by time, marked by an enigmatic symbol she couldn't decipher.

The trees seemed to close in around her, their gnarled branches reaching out like skeletal fingers. The forest floor was littered with fallen leaves and twigs, each step causing them to crunch ominously beneath her boots. Eliza felt a growing sense of anticipation and dread as she ventured deeper into the woods, guided only by the dim light of her flashlight and the map's cryptic directions.

After what felt like hours of navigating through the oppressive darkness, the dense foliage began to thin. Eliza pushed aside a final curtain of vines and emerged into a clearing. Before her lay the Lost City of Dreams, its silhouette rising from the mist like a mirage. Ancient, crumbling buildings with ornate facades loomed against the night sky, their once-majestic architecture now weathered and partially obscured by thick vines and overgrowth.

Eliza's breath caught in her throat as she took in the sight. The city was unlike anything she had ever seen—its streets and alleyways twisted in impossible angles, creating a disorienting maze of paths and structures. The air was filled with an eerie, otherworldly silence, broken only by the occasional distant echo of what might have been a whisper or a sigh.

Determined to explore, Eliza stepped into the city, her flashlight beam dancing over the ancient stonework. As she walked, she noticed peculiar carvings and symbols etched into the walls, many of which resembled those on the orb and the map. It was as if the city itself was a giant puzzle, each building and street holding a piece of the larger mystery.

The deeper Eliza ventured, the more the city seemed to come alive. The shadows lengthened and shifted, playing tricks on her eyes. Statues of forgotten deities and mythological creatures stood sentinel, their eyes seeming to follow her every move. The oppressive silence was occasionally pierced by a faint, melodic chime that seemed to emanate from the very stones of the city.

Suddenly, a soft, ghostly light appeared at the end of a narrow alleyway. Eliza felt a shiver run down her spine as she approached the source of the light. As she rounded the corner, she found herself in a small, open square dominated by an enormous, ancient fountain. The fountain was dry and overgrown with moss, but the light seemed to be emanating from a series of floating orbs hovering above it.

The orbs moved gracefully in the air, casting shimmering reflections on the surrounding buildings. Eliza approached cautiously, her heart racing with a mixture of fear and curiosity. The orbs seemed to respond to her presence, their light intensifying as she drew near. As she reached out to touch one of the orbs, a sudden gust of wind swept through the square, extinguishing the light and plunging the area into darkness.

Eliza's flashlight flickered wildly before going out completely. She was left in complete darkness, her only source of light now the faint glow from the distant moon. Panic began to rise within her as she fumbled with her flashlight, trying to get it to work. The silence was now interrupted by soft, eerie whispers that seemed to come from all directions.

A cold hand clasped her shoulder, and Eliza spun around, her breath hitching in her throat. She expected to see an intruder or a phantom, but there was nothing—only the oppressive darkness and the unsettling whispers. Her flashlight blinked back to life, revealing a tall figure standing in the shadows. The figure was cloaked in a dark robe, its face obscured by a hood.

"Eliza Thornfield," the figure spoke in a voice that was both commanding and soothing. "You have ventured far into the heart of the city. What do you seek?"

Eliza's mind raced. She had not expected to encounter anyone, let alone someone who seemed to know her name. "I'm looking for the truth," she replied, her voice steadier than she felt. "The truth about the orb and the city. What is this place?"

The figure stepped closer, the hood falling slightly to reveal a pair of piercing eyes. "The Lost City of Dreams is a place of power and mystery," the figure said. "It was built by those who sought to harness the creative potential of the universe. But beware, for this city does not easily reveal its secrets."

Eliza felt a chill as the figure's words echoed in the empty square. "What do you know about the orb?" she asked.

The figure's eyes glinted in the dim light. "The orb you carry is a key," they said. "A key to unlocking the greatest mysteries of this city. But it is also a burden. Many have sought its power, only to be consumed by it."

Eliza's heart raced. "What must I do?" she asked, desperation creeping into her voice.

The figure raised a hand, pointing to a distant structure shrouded in darkness. "Follow the path of the orbs," they said. "It will lead you to the heart of the city. There, you will find what you seek. But beware, for the city is alive, and it will test your resolve."

Before Eliza could ask any more questions, the figure vanished into the shadows, leaving her alone in the eerie silence of the square. She took a deep breath and turned toward the dark structure the figure had pointed to. With renewed determination, she set off, the whispers of the city growing louder in her ears.

As she walked, the city seemed to shift and change around her. The buildings twisted and turned, creating a labyrinthine maze that challenged her sense of direction. Each corner she turned led to new and more bizarre configurations of streets and alleys, as if the city itself was actively trying to mislead her.

Despite the growing sense of dread, Eliza pressed on, her flashlight guiding her through the ever-changing landscape. The whispers grew louder, forming a chorus of disembodied voices that seemed to urge her forward. Her steps quickened as she approached the heart of the city, the anticipation of uncovering the truth pushing her onward.

With every step, the air grew colder and the darkness deeper. Eliza knew that the true challenge was yet to come, and the city's secrets were waiting to be uncovered. As she neared the dark structure, she could feel the weight of her quest pressing down on her, but she was determined to face whatever lay ahead.

The Lost City of Dreams held its secrets close, but Eliza was ready to unravel its mysteries. Her journey had just begun, and the path ahead was fraught with danger and intrigue.

4

The Labyrinth of Echoes

Eliza's footsteps echoed through the labyrinthine corridors of the dark structure, the chilling silence amplifying every sound in the cold, oppressive air. The architecture of the building was both grand and grotesque, with towering columns and arches that seemed to stretch infinitely. The stone walls were covered in faded murals and cryptic symbols, their meanings lost to the ages but still imbued with a sense of ancient power.

Her flashlight's beam cut through the darkness, revealing a vast, open chamber that stretched out before her. The floor was littered with debris— crumbled stone, shards of glass, and fragments of broken statues. The only source of light came from the dim glow of the orb, which Eliza had kept close, its light flickering ominously with each step she took.

As she moved further into the chamber, the whispers from earlier began to rise again, growing louder and more insistent. They seemed to come from all directions, a cacophony of disembodied voices that wove together into an unsettling symphony. The whispers carried a sense of urgency, as though they were warning her of something—or perhaps guiding her.

In the center of the chamber stood an enormous stone archway, adorned with elaborate carvings and glowing faintly with an eerie, phosphorescent light. Eliza approached it cautiously, her senses heightened. The archway was framed by two statues of mythical creatures—beasts with lion-like bodies and serpent heads—whose eyes seemed to follow her every movement.

Eliza's flashlight revealed a series of ancient inscriptions around the archway, the same symbols she had seen on the orb and the map. She felt a shiver as the orb's glow intensified, casting long, undulating shadows on the walls. It was as if the archway was reacting to her presence.

Taking a deep breath, Eliza stepped through the archway, her heart pounding with anticipation. Beyond it lay a new corridor, its walls lined with mirrors that reflected her image back at her in a fractured, disorienting manner. The mirrors seemed to ripple and shimmer, creating the illusion of movement and depth. Each step she took felt as though she were walking deeper into a dream—or perhaps a nightmare.

As she continued, the whispers grew louder, now accompanied by faint, eerie music that seemed to emanate from the mirrors themselves. The melody was hauntingly beautiful, but it carried an undercurrent of menace that made Eliza's skin crawl. The corridor twisted and turned in impossible angles, and Eliza struggled to keep track of her direction.

The mirrors began to distort her reflections, creating multiple, shifting images of herself. Each reflection seemed to have a life of its own, moving independently and making it difficult to discern which way was forward. Eliza felt a growing sense of disorientation and panic, the labyrinth pressing in on her from all sides.

Suddenly, a loud crash echoed through the corridor, and one of the mirrors shattered, its fragments falling to the ground with a sharp, metallic clatter. Eliza froze, her flashlight beam sweeping across the broken glass. The whispers grew louder, now accompanied by a low, guttural growl that seemed to reverberate through the walls.

From the darkness ahead, a shadowy figure emerged—a tall, gaunt silhouette with hollow eyes. The figure's presence seemed to distort the air around it, making it difficult for Eliza to focus. The whispers turned into a frenzied murmur, and the music became discordant, creating an overwhelming cacophony.

Eliza backed away slowly, her flashlight flickering erratically as she struggled to maintain her composure. The figure advanced, its movements fluid and unnerving. As it drew closer, Eliza could see that it was cloaked in tattered robes, its face obscured by a hood. The figure raised a skeletal hand, and the shadows around it seemed to writhe and twist.

Desperation surged through Eliza as she searched for an escape. She turned and ran, her footsteps pounding against the stone floor. The corridor seemed to stretch endlessly, each turn revealing more mirrors and more distorted reflections. The growls and whispers followed her, growing louder and more insistent with each step.

As she rounded a corner, Eliza stumbled upon a small alcove, its walls lined with ancient, dust-covered books. She ducked into the alcove, trying to catch her breath and regain her bearings. The figure's footsteps grew louder, and she could hear its labored breathing, as if it were struggling to keep pace.

Eliza grabbed one of the books and opened it, hoping to find something useful. The pages were filled with arcane symbols and illustrations, but nothing that seemed immediately relevant. She felt a surge of frustration and fear, knowing that time was running out.

Just then, a loud crash echoed through the corridor, and the shadowy figure's growls turned into a howl of rage. The mirrors shattered, and the corridor seemed to collapse in on itself, the walls closing in and trapping Eliza in the alcove. The whispers became a deafening roar, and the ground shook violently.

With a final, desperate effort, Eliza grabbed a handful of the broken mirror shards and hurled them at the advancing figure. The shards struck the figure, causing it to recoil and dissolve into a cloud of dark mist. The roar of the whispers faded, and the shaking subsided, leaving Eliza in a tense, suffocating silence.

Breathing heavily, Eliza stepped out of the alcove, her flashlight beam cutting through the darkness. The corridor was now eerily still, the mirrors shattered and scattered across the floor. She could see the archway she had entered from, and beyond it, the vast chamber with the ancient statues.

Eliza made her way back to the archway, her heart still racing from the encounter. She knew that the labyrinth had been a test—a trial designed to challenge her resolve and courage. As she emerged from the archway, she took a moment to steady herself, her thoughts racing with the implications of what she had just experienced.

The Lost City of Dreams was more than just a place of mystery; it was a living, breathing entity that reacted to those who dared to uncover its secrets. Eliza understood that her journey was far from over, and the challenges ahead would test her even further.

With renewed determination, she set her sights on the next phase of her quest. The labyrinth had revealed the depths of the city's mysteries, but it had also shown her the strength she possessed. Eliza was ready to face whatever lay ahead, knowing that the true adventure had only just begun.

5

The Chamber of Whispers

Eliza's footsteps echoed through the cavernous halls of the Lost City as she navigated her way through a dimly lit passageway. The oppressive silence of the labyrinth had been replaced by a faint, rhythmic humming that seemed to reverberate through the very walls. Her flashlight flickered sporadically, casting erratic shadows that danced along the ancient stone walls.

The passage narrowed into a vast chamber, and Eliza's breath caught in her throat as she stepped into the open space. The Chamber of Whispers was unlike anything she had encountered so far—an enormous, circular room with a high, domed ceiling that was adorned with intricate mosaics and arcane symbols. The floor was covered in a thick layer of dust, and the air was heavy with the scent of must and decay.

In the center of the chamber stood a grand, circular pedestal, its surface engraved with more of the mysterious symbols that had become all too familiar to Eliza. The pedestal was surrounded by a series of ancient statues, their eyes hollow and their expressions frozen in eerie grimaces. The statues seemed to be guarding something, but what that was remained hidden in the shadows.

Eliza approached the pedestal cautiously, her senses heightened by the oppressive atmosphere. As she neared it, the rhythmic humming grew louder, filling the chamber with a haunting melody. The sound was both beautiful and unsettling, a delicate balance that created an atmosphere of foreboding.

On the pedestal was a small, ornate box—similar in design to the one she had found the orb in, but intricately decorated with gold filigree and set with precious gemstones. The box's surface was covered in complex patterns and runes that seemed to shift and change as the light from her flashlight played over them. It was clear that the box was significant, possibly holding the key to the next stage of her quest.

Eliza reached out to touch the box, but as her fingers brushed against its surface, the humming stopped abruptly. The chamber was plunged into a deafening silence, broken only by the sound of her own ragged breathing. She felt a shiver run down her spine as the temperature in the room dropped suddenly, the air growing cold and heavy.

A low, rumbling noise emanated from the walls, and Eliza turned to see the statues beginning to move. Their stone limbs creaked and groaned as they shifted into more menacing poses, their eyes glowing with a malevolent light. The statues' expressions twisted into snarls, and their once-innocuous gazes now seemed to follow her every move.

Eliza's heart raced as she backed away from the pedestal, her flashlight flickering wildly. The rhythmic humming returned, now distorted and more discordant, creating a sense of impending danger. The walls of the chamber began to close in, the ceiling lowering slowly and ominously. It was clear that the chamber was designed to test and challenge those who dared to enter.

As the statues advanced, their movements slow but deliberate, Eliza knew she had to act quickly. She needed to figure out the purpose of the box and find a way to escape the chamber before it was too late. With trembling hands, she examined the intricate patterns and runes on the box, trying to decipher their meaning.

The runes seemed to glow faintly in response to her touch, and Eliza noticed that they matched some of the symbols on the orb. She recalled the whispers she had heard earlier—their rhythmic pattern and haunting melody. It dawned on her that the key to unlocking the box might lie in the chamber's strange music.

Eliza took a deep breath and began to hum the melody she had heard earlier, trying to match the rhythm and tone as closely as possible. As she hummed, she watched the box closely for any signs of change. The runes on its surface seemed to respond to the music, their glow intensifying with each note she sang.

The statues paused in their advance, their glowing eyes fixed on her as she continued to hum. The rhythmic humming from the chamber grew louder and more harmonious, blending with her own voice to create a haunting, ethereal sound. The pedestal began to vibrate slightly, and Eliza could feel a subtle energy building in the air.

Suddenly, the box began to open, its lid creaking as it revealed its contents. Inside was a delicate, silver key, its surface engraved with more of the mysterious symbols. The key seemed to pulse with a soft, inner light, and Eliza felt a surge of hope and excitement. This key was clearly important, and it was likely the next piece of the puzzle.

As Eliza reached for the key, the statues resumed their advance, their movements becoming more urgent. The ceiling continued to lower, and the walls seemed to close in, leaving Eliza with a growing sense of urgency. She grabbed the key and turned to face the chamber's exit, but the path was now blocked by a thick, impenetrable barrier.

In a panic, Eliza looked around the chamber for another way out. Her flashlight's beam revealed a series of hidden alcoves along the walls, each containing more of the enigmatic symbols. She realized that the key might be used to unlock one of these alcoves, potentially providing an escape route.

With the statues closing in, Eliza sprinted towards the nearest alcove, her breath coming in short, desperate gasps. She inserted the key into a small, hidden lock on the alcove's door, her hands shaking as she turned it. The lock clicked open, and the door swung wide to reveal a narrow passageway.

Eliza dashed through the passageway, the sound of the statues' movements growing fainter behind her. The passage was dark and narrow, with the walls lined with more of the shifting symbols and runes. She followed the passage, hoping it would lead her to safety.

After what felt like an eternity, the passage opened into another chamber, smaller and less ominous than the previous one. The chamber was filled with ancient artifacts and scrolls, their surfaces covered in dust. In the center of the room stood a pedestal with an ancient tome, its cover adorned with the same symbols she had encountered throughout the city.

Eliza approached the pedestal and carefully opened the tome. The pages were filled with detailed illustrations and explanations of the symbols, providing insights into the city's mysteries and the purpose of the artifacts. As she read, she began to understand the significance of her journey and the challenges that lay ahead.

With the knowledge gained from the tome, Eliza felt a renewed sense of purpose. The Chamber of Whispers had tested her resolve and ingenuity, but she had emerged victorious. As she prepared to continue her quest, she knew that the Lost City of Dreams held many more secrets, and she was determined to uncover them all.

6

The Echoing Vault

Eliza emerged from the narrow passageway into a dimly lit cavern, her flashlight casting long, eerie shadows across the rough-hewn walls. The air was thick with the musty odor of damp earth and old stone. She took a moment to steady her breath, her heart still racing from the harrowing escape through the labyrinthine passageways.

The cavern was vast, with a high, vaulted ceiling that disappeared into darkness. Stalactites hung like jagged teeth from above, and the ground was uneven, covered with loose gravel and scattered boulders. In the center of the cavern stood a massive, ancient door, its surface adorned with intricate carvings and symbols that pulsed with a faint, otherworldly light.

Eliza approached the door cautiously, her eyes scanning the carvings for any sign of a mechanism or lock. The symbols on the door matched those she had seen in the tome she had discovered, hinting at a deeper connection between the city's artifacts and the trials she had faced. The light from her flashlight illuminated the carvings, revealing a depiction of a complex mechanism that seemed to be part of the door's locking system.

The rhythmic hum from earlier seemed to resonate within the cavern, amplifying the sense of unease that Eliza felt. She could hear faint echoes of her own movements, creating a disorienting effect that made it difficult to gauge the source of the sounds. The cavern seemed alive with whispers and murmurs, as if the walls themselves were trying to communicate.

Eliza examined the carvings more closely, noting that they resembled the patterns she had encountered in the Chamber of Whispers. She recalled the tome's description of the symbols and their functions. According to the text, the door could only be opened by aligning the symbols in a specific sequence, a process that required solving a complex puzzle.

With renewed determination, Eliza began to manipulate the symbols on the door, pressing and turning them in various combinations. As she worked, the hum in the cavern grew louder and more insistent, and the air around her seemed to vibrate with an unseen energy. She could feel the tension mounting, as if the cavern itself were watching her every move.

The door's carvings began to shift and change in response to her actions, revealing hidden compartments and mechanisms. Eliza's hands moved with precision, guided by her knowledge of the tome and her instincts. Each successful alignment of the symbols triggered a soft, melodic chime that echoed through the cavern, adding to the eerie atmosphere.

Despite her progress, the cavern's whispers grew more chaotic, and the shadows around her seemed to twist and writhe. Eliza felt a growing sense of urgency, as though the cavern was actively trying to thwart her efforts. The echoes of her movements became more pronounced, and she could hear faint, distant footsteps that seemed to come from every direction.

Just as she was about to complete the final sequence, a deafening crash reverberated through the cavern. Eliza spun around, her flashlight beam cutting through the darkness to reveal a new threat—a large, stone monolith that had descended from the ceiling and now blocked the entrance to the cavern. The monolith was covered in the same symbols as the door, its surface emitting a low, ominous glow.

Panic surged through Eliza as she realized that the monolith was closing off her escape route. She needed to finish the puzzle quickly or risk being trapped in the cavern forever. She redoubled her efforts, working with renewed focus and determination. The whispers grew louder, merging into a cacophony of voices that seemed to mock her efforts.

As she completed the final alignment of the symbols, the door began to creak and groan, its massive frame slowly sliding open to reveal a hidden chamber beyond. Eliza could see a faint, pulsing light emanating from within the chamber, and she felt a surge of relief as she realized she had succeeded in unlocking the door.

With a final glance at the now stationary monolith, Eliza stepped through the open door into the hidden chamber. The chamber was filled with an assortment of ancient artifacts and relics, their surfaces shimmering with a soft, ethereal light. At the center of the chamber stood a pedestal, atop which rested an intricately crafted amulet.

The amulet was adorned with a large, multifaceted gem that seemed to change color and intensity with every flicker of light. Eliza approached the pedestal, her heart racing with anticipation. She could sense that the amulet was a key component in her quest, and she was determined to uncover its secrets.

As she reached for the amulet, a sudden chill swept through the chamber, and the shadows seemed to come alive, swirling and coalescing into a formidable, spectral figure. The figure's presence filled the chamber with an oppressive energy, and Eliza felt an overwhelming sense of dread.

The spectral figure was cloaked in tattered robes, its face obscured by a hood.

Its eyes glowed with an eerie light, and its voice echoed with a haunting, otherworldly tone. "You have trespassed into the Echoing Vault," the figure intoned. "Only those who prove their worth may claim the amulet."

Eliza stood her ground, her resolve unwavering despite the figure's menacing presence. She had come too far to turn back now, and she knew that the amulet was crucial to her quest. With a steady voice, she spoke, "I am here to uncover the truth and to find the answers that lie within this city. I will not be deterred."

The spectral figure's eyes glowed brighter, and the chamber seemed to fill with a swirling mist. The whispers and echoes grew louder, converging into a single, resonant voice that filled the space with a sense of foreboding. The figure raised its hand, and the mist began to coalesce into a series of challenging illusions and obstacles.

Eliza's heart pounded as she faced the illusions, each one more daunting than the last. She had to navigate a series of complex trials and challenges, testing her intellect, bravery, and resolve. With each trial she overcame, the spectral figure's presence seemed to wane, and the chamber's oppressive atmosphere began to lift.

Finally, after what felt like an eternity, Eliza stood before the pedestal once more, the amulet within her grasp. The spectral figure had vanished, and the chamber was filled with a renewed sense of calm and tranquility. Eliza carefully picked up the amulet, feeling its power resonate through her.

With the amulet in hand, Eliza knew that she had taken another significant step in her journey through the Lost City of Dreams. The Echoing Vault had tested her to her limits, but she had emerged victorious. As she prepared to leave the chamber, she felt a renewed sense of purpose and determination.

The Lost City still held many secrets, but Eliza was now one step closer to uncovering the truth. The challenges ahead would be even greater, but she was ready to face whatever lay in her path. The Echoing Vault had shown her the strength and courage she possessed, and she was determined to continue her quest with unwavering resolve.

7

The Shattered Mirror

The amulet's soft glow provided Eliza with just enough light as she navigated the narrow, winding corridor that followed the Echoing Vault. The cavern's oppressive darkness had given way to a labyrinthine network of tunnels, each twisting and turning in seemingly random directions. Eliza could feel the weight of the amulet around her neck, its power a constant reminder of the challenges still ahead.

The corridor opened into a large, circular room, its walls lined with shards of glass that caught and reflected the faint light of the amulet. The floor was covered in a thick layer of dust, disturbed only by her own footprints. The room was eerily silent, the air thick with a sense of anticipation.

In the center of the room stood an ornate, antique mirror, its frame intricately carved with symbols and designs that matched those of the previous trials. The mirror's surface was shattered, with cracks running through it like spiderwebs. Despite its damaged state, the mirror seemed to radiate an unsettling energy.

Eliza approached the mirror cautiously, her reflection distorted and fragmented by the numerous cracks. She could see glimpses of her own face, each one twisted and contorted into an array of grotesque expressions. The shattered glass created a disorienting effect, making it difficult to focus on any single point.

As Eliza examined the mirror, a low, rumbling sound filled the room. She turned to see the shards of glass beginning to shift and rearrange themselves, forming a series of images and patterns. The images depicted scenes from her past, memories she had long since buried. They flickered and danced across the fractured surface, each one more vivid and painful than the last.

Eliza's heart raced as she saw scenes from her childhood—her family, her friends, and moments of joy and sorrow. The memories seemed to come alive, their emotional weight palpable. She could hear the echoes of laughter, arguments, and tears, each sound amplified by the mirror's reflections.

The mirror's images began to shift, morphing into a nightmarish tableau of her deepest fears and regrets. Faces of people she had lost, failures she had endured, and decisions she wished she could change all converged in a chaotic swirl. The room's temperature dropped suddenly, and a cold, damp mist began to envelop the space.

Eliza felt a rising sense of panic as the reflections became more distorted and menacing. The mirror seemed to be alive, its shattered surface forming a distorted, mocking version of her own image. The shards of glass began to pulse with an eerie light, creating an unsettling rhythm that reverberated through the room.

In a desperate attempt to make sense of the mirror's purpose, Eliza reached out and touched the glass. As her fingers made contact, a jolt of electricity surged through her, and the images in the mirror froze. The room was plunged into darkness, the only light coming from the faint glow of the amulet around her neck.

The darkness was suffocating, and Eliza felt a sense of isolation and despair. She could hear faint whispers in the void, their voices distorted and echoing. The whispers seemed to taunt her, highlighting her insecurities and fears. She tried to focus, but the oppressive darkness made it difficult to think clearly.

Suddenly, a blinding flash of light erupted from the mirror, illuminating the room and revealing a hidden compartment behind the shattered glass. The compartment was filled with an assortment of strange, otherworldly objects—crystals, scrolls, and artifacts that seemed to hum with an unknown energy.

Eliza approached the compartment, her hands trembling as she reached for one of the objects. It was a small, crystalline orb, its surface smooth and reflective. The orb seemed to resonate with the same energy as the amulet, and Eliza felt a surge of hope and determination.

As she picked up the orb, the mirror's surface began to shift and reform, the shattered fragments aligning themselves into a new pattern. The images of her past and fears dissolved, replaced by a clearer, more cohesive reflection of herself. The mirror's surface now showed her as she truly was—brave, resilient, and determined.

Eliza took a deep breath and examined the crystalline orb more closely. The orb contained a swirling, luminescent mist that seemed to pulse with a rhythm of its own. She could feel a connection between the orb and the amulet, as though they were two halves of a greater whole.

With the orb in hand, Eliza felt a renewed sense of purpose. She realized that the mirror was not just a test of her fears and regrets, but a reflection of her inner strength and resilience. The shattered glass had been a metaphor for the challenges she faced, and the orb represented the clarity and resolve she needed to continue her journey.

As she prepared to leave the room, the shattered mirror began to emit a soft, melodic hum, its surface glowing with a warm, inviting light. The once-oppressive atmosphere had lifted, replaced by a sense of calm and acceptance. The room's temperature returned to normal, and the mist dissipated, leaving Eliza with a newfound sense of clarity and determination.

Eliza exited the room with the crystalline orb and the amulet, her mind filled with a sense of purpose and resolve. The Shattered Mirror had tested her deeply, forcing her to confront her fears and insecurities. But she had emerged stronger and more focused, ready to face whatever challenges lay ahead in the Lost City of Dreams.

As she continued her journey, Eliza felt a renewed sense of confidence. The trials had shown her the strength and resilience she possessed, and she was determined to uncover the secrets of the city and fulfill her quest. The Shattered Mirror had been a turning point in her journey, and she was ready to face the next challenge with unwavering resolve.

8

The Phantom's Labyrinth

**Chapter 8:

 Eliza stepped into the narrow corridor that led from the Shattered Mirror room, her footsteps echoing against the stone walls. The crystalline orb hung from her neck, casting a soft, pulsating light that barely illuminated the path ahead. She could still feel the eerie calm of the mirror room lingering, a strange contrast to the disquieting stillness of her current surroundings.

The corridor twisted and turned in seemingly random directions, its walls lined with ancient inscriptions that glowed faintly in the orb's light. The air was thick and heavy, filled with an unsettling quiet that seemed to press in from all sides. Eliza moved cautiously, her senses heightened, acutely aware that the labyrinth she now faced was unlike any she had encountered before.

As she rounded a corner, the corridor opened into a vast chamber. The space was dominated by an elaborate maze of towering walls, constructed from dark stone and adorned with intricate patterns and symbols. The walls of the maze seemed to shift and waver, as if alive, and the chamber was filled with a low, constant hum that seemed to vibrate through the stone.

Eliza's gaze was drawn to a small pedestal situated in the center of the chamber. Atop the pedestal rested an ornate key, its surface encrusted with gemstones that reflected the faint light of her orb. The key was a striking contrast to the somber surroundings, its brilliance a beacon of hope amidst the darkness.

However, as she took a step toward the pedestal, the walls of the maze began to move. They shifted with a slow, deliberate motion, rearranging themselves and altering the maze's layout. The once straightforward path was now a complex network of twisting passages and dead ends. Eliza realized that the maze was not a static structure but a dynamic, shifting labyrinth designed to disorient and confound.

Determined to retrieve the key, Eliza cautiously entered the maze. The walls around her seemed to close in, the shifting patterns creating a disorienting effect that made it difficult to gauge her surroundings. The hum in the chamber grew louder, vibrating through her bones, and the maze's walls seemed to pulse with an eerie, malevolent energy.

Eliza navigated the maze with a mixture of intuition and careful observation. She used the orb's light to illuminate the inscriptions on the walls, hoping they might provide clues or guidance. The inscriptions were cryptic, their meanings obscured by layers of ancient language and symbolism. Despite her efforts, the maze remained a treacherous puzzle.

As she ventured deeper into the labyrinth, Eliza began to hear faint, ghostly whispers. The whispers seemed to come from every direction, their words indistinguishable but filled with a sense of urgency and dread. The whispers grew louder, becoming a cacophony of voices that seemed to mock her efforts and amplify her fears.

The labyrinth's walls continued to shift, and Eliza found herself trapped in a series of dead ends and loops. The shifting paths made it difficult to retrace her steps, and the maze's ever-changing layout seemed to conspire against her. She felt a growing sense of frustration and unease, the whispers growing more insistent and the hum more oppressive.

Suddenly, the maze walls began to close in, narrowing the passages and creating a sense of claustrophobic pressure. Eliza's heart raced as she realized that the labyrinth was not just a test of navigation but also a trial of endurance. The walls seemed to be closing in on her, forcing her to move quickly and decisively.

In her desperation, Eliza took a deep breath and focused on the inscriptions on the walls. She noticed that the symbols seemed to form a repeating pattern, and she began to follow the pattern, hoping it would lead her to the correct path. Her movements were precise and deliberate, guided by her knowledge of the inscriptions and her instinctive sense of direction.

As she followed the pattern, the maze walls began to shift again, creating a new pathway that led toward the pedestal. The whispers grew quieter, and the oppressive hum of the chamber began to recede. Eliza moved with renewed determination, her goal clear in her mind.

Finally, she reached the pedestal and the ornate key. She carefully picked up the key, its weight and cold metal a reassuring contrast to the maze's oppressive atmosphere. As she held the key, the maze walls began to recede, their shifting patterns returning to their original positions.

Eliza turned to leave the chamber, the key clutched tightly in her hand. The whispers had faded, replaced by a sense of calm and accomplishment. The labyrinth had tested her resolve and resourcefulness, but she had emerged victorious.

As she exited the chamber, Eliza felt a renewed sense of purpose. The Phantom's Labyrinth had been a formidable challenge, but it had also revealed her inner strength and determination. The key was a crucial component of her journey, and she knew that the next steps in her quest would be even more demanding.

With the key securely in her possession, Eliza continued her journey through the Lost City of Dreams. The trials she had faced so far had prepared her for the challenges ahead, and she was ready to confront whatever lay in her path. The Phantom's Labyrinth had been a pivotal moment in her quest, and she was determined to see it through to the end.

9

The Heart of Shadows

Eliza moved through the darkened corridors of the Lost City with a sense of urgency. The key she had retrieved from the Phantom's Labyrinth hung heavy around her neck, a constant reminder of the obstacles she had overcome. The city's atmosphere had become increasingly oppressive, and the shadows seemed to grow darker and more menacing with each step she took.

Her path led her to a grand archway, its surface covered in intricate carvings that matched those of the labyrinth and the mirror. The archway opened into a vast, cavernous chamber, its floor littered with rubble and debris. The air was thick with an unsettling silence, and the temperature had dropped noticeably, creating an eerie chill that seeped into her bones.

The chamber's ceiling was lost in darkness, and the walls were adorned with large, swirling patterns that seemed to writhe and shift as if alive. The only source of light came from the key, its surface emitting a faint, pulsating glow that cast long, wavering shadows across the chamber. Eliza could feel an almost tangible sense of dread emanating from the space, as though the very walls were holding their breath.

At the center of the chamber stood a massive stone altar, its surface covered in strange symbols and markings. Above the altar, suspended from the ceiling by thick chains, was a large, obsidian orb. The orb glowed with a sinister, dark light, and Eliza could feel a malevolent energy radiating from it. The aura of the orb was so intense that it seemed to drain the light from the chamber, leaving only a shadowy haze.

Eliza approached the altar cautiously, her footsteps muffled by the thick layer of dust on the floor. The symbols on the altar matched those she had seen throughout the city, and she could sense that the orb was a key element in the city's mysteries. Her heart pounded in her chest as she reached the altar, the key clutched tightly in her hand.

As she examined the symbols, she realized that they formed a complex pattern, a puzzle that needed to be solved to unlock the orb. The markings on the altar seemed to correspond to the patterns she had encountered in the previous trials. Eliza's mind raced as she tried to decipher the puzzle, her thoughts interrupted by the growing sense of unease in the chamber.

The shadows around the chamber began to coalesce, forming indistinct shapes and figures that flickered and danced at the edges of her vision. The temperature dropped further, and Eliza could see her breath in the cold air. The dark figures moved closer, their forms becoming more defined and menacing. They seemed to be drawn to the orb, their presence an ominous sign of the power it contained.

As Eliza worked to solve the puzzle, the figures grew more insistent, their forms becoming clearer and more defined. They were ghostly apparitions, their eyes glowing with an otherworldly light. The apparitions moved with a purpose, their ethereal forms drifting closer to the altar. Eliza could feel their cold presence brushing against her, their whispers mingling with the eerie silence of the chamber.

Determined not to be distracted, Eliza focused on the symbols on the altar. She noticed that some of the markings seemed to respond to her touch, shifting and changing in response to her movements. She worked with careful precision, aligning the symbols in what she hoped was the correct sequence.

As she completed the pattern, the orb above the altar began to glow more intensely, its dark light casting long, writhing shadows across the chamber. The apparitions grew agitated, their movements becoming more erratic and desperate. Eliza could hear their whispers growing louder, a cacophony of voices that seemed to merge into a single, resonant tone.

The shadows in the chamber began to swirl and converge, forming a swirling vortex of darkness that seemed to draw the energy from the orb. The vortex expanded, its presence filling the chamber with a suffocating pressure. Eliza could feel the intense energy radiating from the vortex, and she struggled to maintain her focus.

With a final, decisive movement, Eliza completed the puzzle. The orb's dark light flared brightly, and the shadows around the chamber began to recede. The vortex of darkness dissipated, leaving the chamber in a state of uneasy calm. The apparitions vanished, their presence replaced by a haunting silence.

Eliza's breath came in ragged gasps as she looked at the orb. It now glowed with a soft, steady light, and the malevolent energy that had pervaded the chamber seemed to have dissipated. The symbols on the altar had settled into a new pattern, one that seemed to hint at the path forward in her journey.

She carefully removed the orb from its chains, its weight heavy in her hands. The orb was now a source of light and energy, its dark power transformed into something more manageable. Eliza knew that this was a crucial moment in her quest, and she felt a renewed sense of determination.

As she prepared to leave the chamber, she glanced back at the altar and the symbols. The Heart of Shadows had tested her resolve and strength, and she had emerged victorious. The orb was a powerful artifact, and its significance to her journey was clear.

With the orb in hand, Eliza continued her journey through the Lost City of Dreams. The challenges she had faced in the Heart of Shadows had tested her courage and resourcefulness, but she was ready to confront whatever lay ahead. The orb's light guided her path, and she was determined to uncover the city's deepest secrets and fulfill her quest.

The Heart of Shadows had been a pivotal moment in her journey, and Eliza was prepared to face the next challenge with unwavering resolve. The trials she had faced had forged her into a stronger and more capable adventurer, and she was ready to embrace whatever mysteries and dangers lay ahead in the enigmatic Lost City of Dreams.

10

The Echoing Abyss

The corridor leading from the Heart of Shadows was as oppressive as ever, with walls that seemed to pulse and shift under the dim light of Eliza's orb. Each step she took felt heavier than the last, as if the very air was resisting her progress. She could feel the weight of her previous trials pressing down on her, adding to the mounting tension she felt as she ventured deeper into the Lost City of Dreams.

Her path eventually led her to a heavy, ancient door, its surface engraved with a complex array of runes and symbols. The door was adorned with deep grooves that glowed faintly in the light, casting eerie shadows across the corridor. Eliza approached the door with a mixture of anticipation and apprehension, the orb's light flickering as she examined the intricate designs.

With a deep breath, Eliza pushed against the door. It creaked open with a groan, revealing a vast, cavernous space beyond. The room was enormous, its ceiling lost in the darkness above. The floor was a seemingly endless expanse of jagged rock, and the walls were lined with ancient carvings that glowed with a dim, unsettling light.

As Eliza stepped into the room, she was struck by the sheer scale of the space. The floor was littered with debris, and the air was thick with a palpable sense of foreboding. The only sound was a low, rhythmic hum that seemed to emanate from the very heart of the cavern.

The cavern's center was dominated by a massive, swirling vortex of shadow. The vortex pulsed and roiled with an ominous energy, its surface churning like a stormy sea. The shadows within the vortex seemed to writhe and twist, forming dark, indistinct shapes that flickered in and out of view. Eliza could feel a strong, almost magnetic pull emanating from the vortex, drawing her towards it.

Despite her resolve, Eliza could not help but feel a deep sense of dread as she approached the vortex. The air grew colder, and the rhythmic hum grew louder, resonating through her body. The shadows within the vortex seemed to reach out towards her, their dark tendrils stretching and curling as if attempting to grasp her.

Eliza took a cautious step forward, her heart pounding in her chest. The vortex seemed to respond to her presence, its energy surging with an intensity that made the chamber's air vibrate. The rhythmic hum became a deafening roar, filling the space with an overwhelming sound that made it difficult to think clearly.

Suddenly, the shadows within the vortex began to coalesce into distinct forms. Ghostly figures emerged from the swirling darkness, their eyes glowing with an otherworldly light. The figures were ethereal and insubstantial, their forms shifting and changing with each passing moment. They moved with a fluid grace, their movements eerily synchronized with the rhythm of the vortex.

Eliza could feel the weight of the figures' gaze upon her, their presence a constant, oppressive force. The figures seemed to be watching her every move, their glowing eyes reflecting a mixture of curiosity and malevolence. The air around her grew colder, and she could see her breath fogging in the icy atmosphere.

Determined to press on, Eliza approached the vortex with caution. The swirling shadows seemed to part and shift as she neared, forming a narrow path that led deeper into the darkness. The path was lined with more of the eerie, glowing runes, their light casting long, wavering shadows across the floor.

As she moved along the path, the vortex's energy grew more intense, creating a palpable sense of pressure that made it difficult to breathe. The rhythmic hum had become a steady, pulsing beat that seemed to synchronize with her heartbeat. The shadows within the vortex continued to swirl and twist, their movements becoming more erratic and chaotic.

Eliza reached the center of the vortex, where a massive, ancient pedestal stood. Atop the pedestal rested a small, ornate box, its surface covered in intricate carvings and symbols. The box seemed to pulse with a faint, dark light, and Eliza could feel its energy resonating with the vortex's rhythm.

With a deep breath, Eliza approached the pedestal and carefully lifted the box. The moment her hands made contact with it, the vortex's energy surged with a violent intensity. The shadows within the vortex seemed to converge and swirl around her, their movements creating a vortex of darkness that threatened to overwhelm her.

Eliza struggled to maintain her footing as the chamber's energy reached a crescendo. The rhythmic hum became a deafening roar, and the shadows surged and twisted with a frenzied intensity. She could feel the weight of the vortex pressing down on her, its dark energy threatening to consume her.

Summoning every ounce of her strength, Eliza held the box tightly and focused on its intricate carvings. She noticed that the symbols on the box matched those on the pedestal and the chamber's walls. With a determined effort, she began to align the symbols, her movements guided by the rhythmic pulse of the vortex.

As she completed the pattern, the vortex's energy began to dissipate. The shadows receded, their forms dissolving into the darkness. The rhythmic hum faded, leaving the chamber in a state of uneasy silence. The pedestal's light dimmed, and the air grew warmer, the oppressive atmosphere lifting.

Eliza took a deep breath and examined the box. Its dark light had transformed into a soft, steady glow, and the carvings on its surface seemed to hold a new significance. She realized that the box was a key element in her journey, its purpose becoming clearer with each passing moment.

As she prepared to leave the chamber, Eliza glanced back at the vortex and the pedestal. The Echoing Abyss had tested her resolve and strength, and she had emerged victorious. The box was a crucial artifact, and she knew that its significance would become even clearer in the trials to come.

With the box in hand, Eliza continued her journey through the Lost City of Dreams. The challenges she had faced in the Echoing Abyss had tested her courage and resourcefulness, and she was ready to confront whatever lay ahead. The box's glow guided her path, and she was determined to uncover the city's deepest secrets and fulfill her quest.

The Echoing Abyss had been a pivotal moment in her journey, and Eliza was prepared to face the next challenge with unwavering resolve. The trials she had faced had forged her into a stronger and more capable adventurer, and she was ready to embrace whatever mysteries and dangers lay ahead in the enigmatic Lost City of Dreams.

11

The Abyssal Choir

Eliza clutched the ornate box tightly as she exited the Echoing Abyss, the chamber's oppressive atmosphere still clinging to her. The labyrinthine corridors of the Lost City twisted and turned in a disorienting pattern, each passageway leading deeper into the heart of the city. The box's soft, steady glow was a comforting presence amid the encroaching darkness, guiding her path.

The city seemed to grow colder as she ventured forward, the shadows stretching long and ominous in the dim light of her orb. The walls around her were lined with faded murals depicting scenes of ancient rituals and long-forgotten ceremonies. The intricate designs seemed to pulse with a life of their own, their colors shifting and changing with each step she took.

Eventually, Eliza came upon a grand archway, its surface adorned with elaborate carvings of mythical creatures and celestial symbols. The archway opened into an enormous hall, its ceiling lost in the depths of darkness. The room was filled with an unsettling quiet, broken only by the faint echoes of her footsteps as she entered.

The hall's floor was a polished expanse of obsidian, reflecting the dim light of her orb with a haunting, mirror-like sheen. The walls were lined with towering statues, their expressions frozen in a perpetual state of anguish. Each statue was draped in tattered, dark robes, and their eyes seemed to follow her every movement with a disquieting intensity.

At the far end of the hall stood a massive, imposing altar. The altar was intricately carved with swirling patterns and dark, enigmatic symbols. Above the altar was a colossal, ancient organ, its pipes stretching high into the darkness above. The organ's keys were worn and dust-covered, and the entire structure seemed to emanate a sense of foreboding.

As Eliza approached the altar, she noticed that the organ's pipes were connected to an array of strange, glowing conduits. The conduits snaked along the walls and floor, converging at various points in the hall. The soft, rhythmic hum of the conduits seemed to resonate with the organ, creating an eerie, dissonant melody that filled the space.

Eliza felt a chill run down her spine as she approached the altar. The air around her seemed to vibrate with the haunting melody, and the temperature in the hall dropped noticeably. The shadows cast by the statues grew darker and more pronounced, their forms twisting and contorting in the dim light.

She noticed that the altar was adorned with a series of slots and compartments, each one etched with more of the enigmatic symbols she had encountered throughout the city. The ornate box she carried seemed to fit perfectly into one of the compartments, its surface aligning with the markings on the altar.

With a sense of trepidation, Eliza carefully placed the box into the compartment. The moment it made contact, the organ's pipes began to resonate with a deep, resonant tone. The conduits flared to life, their glow intensifying and spreading through the hall. The dissonant melody grew louder, its haunting notes reverberating through the chamber.

The statues lining the walls began to move, their eyes glowing with a malevolent light. The robes of the statues rustled and shifted as if stirred by an unseen force. The atmosphere in the hall grew more oppressive, the air thick with an almost tangible sense of dread.

The organ's melody shifted, its notes becoming more complex and discordant. The shadows cast by the statues seemed to writhe and pulse in time with the music, creating an unsettling visual accompaniment to the eerie melody. Eliza could feel the weight of the hall's energy pressing down on her, making it difficult to breathe.

As the melody reached a crescendo, the statues began to emit ghostly, ethereal voices. The voices joined the organ's music, creating a haunting, otherworldly choir that seemed to echo through the very fabric of the hall. The choir's voices were a blend of mournful wails and discordant chants, their words unintelligible but filled with a sense of desperate longing.

Eliza felt herself being drawn into the music, her senses overwhelmed by the haunting melody and the ghostly choir. The voices seemed to speak directly to her, their haunting tones resonating with her deepest fears and anxieties. The chamber's energy grew more intense, the music and voices blending into a dissonant symphony of darkness.

Desperate to regain control, Eliza focused on the symbols on the altar and the markings on the box. She noticed that the symbols seemed to correspond to the music, their patterns shifting and changing in time with the melody. She realized that the music was a key element in unlocking the altar's secrets.

With a deep breath, Eliza began to align the symbols on the altar, matching them with the notes and rhythms of the organ's melody. She worked with a sense of urgency, her movements guided by the music and the rhythmic hum of the conduits. The haunting choir's voices grew more frenetic, their tones merging into a chaotic cacophony.

As she completed the pattern, the organ's music reached a final, triumphant chord. The voices of the choir converged into a single, resonant note, and the shadows in the hall began to recede. The conduits' glow dimmed, and the oppressive atmosphere lifted, replaced by a sense of calm and resolution.

Eliza took a deep breath and examined the altar. The ornate box had unlocked a new compartment, revealing a small, intricately carved key. The key was a beautiful, ornate artifact, its surface adorned with the same symbols and patterns that had guided her through the hall.

With the key in hand, Eliza prepared to leave the hall. The Abyssal Choir had tested her resolve and strength, but she had emerged victorious. The key was a crucial element in her journey, and she knew that its significance would become clearer as she continued her quest.

As she exited the hall, Eliza felt a renewed sense of purpose. The challenges she had faced in the Abyssal Choir had sharpened her skills and deepened her understanding of the city's mysteries. With the key guiding her path, she was ready to confront whatever lay ahead in the enigmatic Lost City of Dreams.

12

The Idea Explorers: Adventures in Creativity

Embark on a journey of imagination and intrigue with "The Idea Explorers: Adventures in Creativity." Follow Eliza and her team as they navigate the enigmatic Lost City of Dreams, a place where every corner hides a new mystery and every artifact holds the key to boundless creativity. From the haunting echoes of the Abyssal Choir to the unsettling revelations of the Mirror's Reflection, each chapter reveals the city's deep secrets and challenges the explorers' ingenuity and resolve. As they decipher ancient symbols, unlock hidden chambers, and confront otherworldly forces, their quest to unravel the city's mysteries becomes a race against time. Will their creative minds and unyielding spirit be enough to master the trials of this mythical realm? Dive into a world where imagination knows no bounds and every idea could change everything.

13

Chapter 13

14

Chapter 14

Milton Keynes UK
Ingram Content Group UK Ltd.
UKHW021032020824
446373UK00013B/475